This journal
belongs to

Marley
2014

Belle City Gifts™
Racine, WI 53403

Belle City Gifts is an imprint of Broadstreet Publishing
www.broadstreetpublishing.com

Travel Journal
© 2014 by Broadstreet Publishing

ISBN 978-1-4245-4906-1

Cover and interior design by Garborg Design Works, Inc.
www.garborgdesign.com

Printed in China

Travel

JOURNAL

BELLE CITY GIFTS

My
Thoughts

My
Thoughts

My
Thoughts

My
Thoughts

My
Thoughts

My
Thoughts

"For my part, I

My
Thoughts

My
Thoughts

My
Thoughts

My
Thoughts

My
Thoughts

My
Thoughts

My
Thoughts

My Thoughts

My
Thoughts

My
Thoughts

My
Thoughts

My
Thoughts

My
Thoughts

My
Thoughts

My
Thoughts

My
Thoughts

My
Thoughts

My
Thoughts

My
Thoughts

My
Thoughts

My
Thoughts

My
Thoughts

My
Thoughts

My
Thoughts

My
Thoughts

"For my part, I

My
Thoughts

For my part, I

My
Thoughts

My
Thoughts

My
Thoughts

My
Thoughts

My
Thoughts

My
Thoughts

"For my part, I

My
Thoughts

My
Thoughts

My
Thoughts

My
Thoughts

My
Thoughts

My
Thoughts

My
Thoughts

My
Thoughts

My
Thoughts

My
Thoughts

My
Thoughts

My
Thoughts

My
Thoughts

My
Thoughts

My
Thoughts

My
Thoughts

My
Thoughts

My
Thoughts

My
Thoughts

My
Thoughts

My
Thoughts

My
Thoughts

For my part, I

My
Thoughts

My
Thoughts

My
Thoughts

My
Thoughts

"For my part, I

My
Thoughts

My
Thoughts

My
Thoughts

My
Thoughts

My
Thoughts

For my part,

My
Thoughts

My
Thoughts

My
Thoughts

My
Thoughts

My
Thoughts

My
Thoughts

My
Thoughts

My
Thoughts

My
Thoughts

My
Thoughts